Fred Pichel

RAPA NUI

RAPA NUI

photographs & text by

FRED PICKER

·

historical summary
by
Thor Heyerdahl

**PADDINGTON
PRESS LTD**

Two Continents Publishing Group
30 East 42nd St., N.Y.C., 10017, N.Y.

Rapa Nui—Easter Island by Fred Picker
with a commentary by Thor Heyerdahl
Copyright © Paddington Press Ltd.—1974
Photographs Copyright ©—1974 Fred Picker
Printed in the U.S.A. by Scroll Press, Danbury, Connecticut.
Published by Paddington Press Ltd
Two Continents Publishing Group
30 East 42nd St., N.Y.C., 10017, N.Y.
ISBN 0-8467-0021-2
L.C. 73-15025

To Harold and Edna Picker

Acknowledgements

I wish to thank Dr. Thor Heyerdahl for checking my text and contributing a superb historical perspective; Dr. Grant McCall, Dr. William Ayers, Victoria Rapahango Tepuku and Father Melchior for so generously sharing their knowledge of the Island; Dr. Edwin Land of The Polaroid Corporation for his generosity and Jon Holmes for his technical advice. I am especially grateful to Paul Caponigro for the guidance he gave me during this project and for the warm friendship I have enjoyed with Paul and his wife Eleanor.

Most of all, my thanks to Lillian Farber. She cheerfully freed me of a thousand details from the making of travel arrangements to the shooing of flies from under my focusing cloth. Finally she unsnarled and clarified this photographers meandering text. Without her encouragement, skill, and perseverance I would not have attempted this book.

Rapa Nui—Easter Island—The Navel of the World. A tiny island with many names and an ever changing face is finally getting within the reach of modern man in the days when he is already groping for the moon. Those of us who saw and described the island a decade or two ago, before rockets soared above the craters of the moon and jets above the stone giants on the volcanic slopes of Easter Island, feel that we have traveled with the heirs of the statue-makers through ages of their history. We feel the need of an up-to-date description of the island, its progress and its problems. With his excellent photographic studies and concise verbal documentation, Fred Picker introduces us in an admirable manner to Easter Island as it is today.

Colla Micheri, Italy
August 18, 1973

Dr. Thor Heyerdahl, Ph.D.

"Everywhere is the wind of heaven; round and above all are boundless sea and sky, infinite space and a great silence. The dweller there is ever listening for he knows not what, feeling unconsciously that he is in the antechamber to something yet more vast which is just beyond his ken."*

*Katherine Scoresby Routledge, The Mystery of Easter Island: The Story of an Expedition (London, 1919).

SOUTH PACIFIC OCEAN

EASTER ISLAND

(ISLA DE PASCUA or RAPA NUI)

From a Chilean Government chart of 1918

Obs. Spot ✛.l.at. 27° 08′ 37″ S. Long. 109° 26′ 10″ W.

H.W.F. & C. Vh. 21 m. Springs rise 5 ft.

SOUNDINGS IN FATHOMS
HEIGHTS IN FEET

S. sand, Sh. shells, St. stones

Natural Scale $\frac{1}{100.000}$

AUTHORITIES
British Admiralty Chart No. 1386
Chilean Chart No. 68
U.S. Hydrographic Office Publications

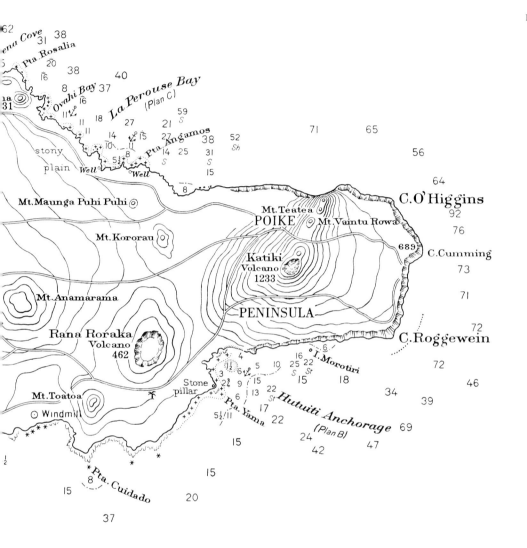

Easter I. Summit. 162° (true) about 35 miles

C. Roggewein
263° (true) about 12 miles

C. O. Higgins

THE LAND

THE LAND

In all the world, there is no place more remote than Rapa Nui—Easter Island. This speck in the Pacific Ocean is located 2,300 miles west of the Chilean coast and its closest neighbor is tiny Pitcairn Island, 1,200 miles still further to the West.

Easter Island does not fit the popular conception of a Polynesian paradise. There are no lush rain forests alive with colorful tropic birds. No coral reef rings the land to provide quiet harbors and clear lagoons. The natural growth is short dry grasses sprouting from dusty red clay. Nowhere on the island are there deposits of moist leaf mold to encourage the growth of rich vegetation. There is an arid harshness to the land that is only tempered by the long sweet shapes of the golden hills.

The atmosphere is not tranquil; there is a strong sensation; a humming pulsation—a secret unknown. The visitor is suspended between the mysterious past and an indefinable atmosphere of vibrating expectancy. The land seems to be waiting—for something.

The shores are precipitous and sown with black lava blocks and outcroppings. Great storm waves with a clear fetch of 2,500 miles have smashed ineffectually against the cliffs since the beginning of time. A view of the shore from any elevated point reveals numerous random explosions as the spray bursts back from the unyielding black armor of the land. The surf is so restless and the rocks so sharp that a swimmer can find only a half dozen places along the entire shore where he can safely enter the water.

There are just two small sand beaches; one open and sunny at Anakena Bay, the other huddled beneath the brooding cliff at Ovahi. Only under certain conditions of wind and sea do either provide a hospitable refuge for an anchored ship or a safe landing place for its boats.

The brutal shores nevertheless enchant the beholder. A marvelous panorama of powerful wave and sparkling spray, brilliant light and flying cloud delights the eye and reflects the moods of man.

The sea provides further bounty—the Nanui, a sweet fish of pure gold and beautiful form—and tuna, and great clawless lobsters. The fruits of the sea fill the hungry belly as its surge and thunder and spray refresh the soul.

Easter Island was born of violence and forged in flame. Eons ago three volcanos burst from the sea to delineate this triangular wedge of land. In the ten mile web of earth stretched between the volcanic cones of Rano Kao, Rano Aroi, and Poike there is an amazing variety of terrain and structure.

Petroglyph of a fish at Anakena

Highlands near Puna Pau

Lower slopes, Poike

A visitor's initial impression depends upon the season and the hour or the part of the island first seen. The most powerful sensation might be of an earth parched until no trace of moisture can be found. There are no springs or streams on the island, and the porous volcanic rock quickly absorbs the erratic rainfall. Rain water gathers only in the crater lakes of Rano Raraku, Rano Kau, and Rano Aroi. There are no other lakes or ponds.

From the dusty red clay the sparse meadow grass sprouts in a range of tones from gold to spring green in response to the rainfall. Over the land millions of black volcanic stones are sprinkled.

The appearance and atmosphere of the landscape changes constantly with the fleeting character of the sky and sea. There are twenty-eight names for different winds and each wind produces peculiarities of cloud and light. The many layers of diversely shaped clouds flow at different rates of speed causing fast moving shadow forms to dart across the land. The cloud-forms can change in seconds from the cottony cumulus of fair weather to the "mackeral skies and mares tails" that cause "tall ships to carry small sails." Rain squalls and howling winds may scourge one part of the island while the remainder bakes beneath the tropic sun. There are flat treeless stony stretches of lunar-like desolation. Smooth rounded hills, sensuous in form, are so symmetrical that it is difficult to believe that they were not made by men. No one is sure that they were not. Peculiar layers of horizontal bands, visible at great distances, follow the contours of the smooth hillsides.

Four thousand horses and ten thousand sheep roam the unfenced range. They and a few cows grow strong on nothing but the spikey dry mineral-rich meadow grass. The little moisture they find is supplemented by visits to the stagnant waters of the crater lakes of Rano Raraku and Rano Aroi. No sea birds nest among the rocks, no song birds interrupt the silence, but small swift hawks ride the wind watching for the tiny movements that betray the presence of prey.

Groups of trees dot the island. Here in a hollow that holds a trace of moisture are a dozen pungent eucalyptus forty feet tall. Banana trees mark the entrances to many of the thousands of serpentine caves that vein the land. A grove of graceful palms crowds the beach of Anakena, while other palms exist alone, like outcasts in improbable places. The strangest of all trees grow in a tight cluster on the very top of Poike. From a distance they look like a tuft of feathers sprouting from the head-dress of an ancient warrior.

Poike

Rangeland at Rano Aroi

The toromiro tree grows only on the crater floor of the volcano Rano Kao. The beautiful close grained wood was used by the first settlers as writing boards to record their activities. The dense wood was formed into the shape of paddle blades called Rongo Rongo and on these they carved strange symbols.

Among the most dramatic features of the land are the great volcanic cones, the largest of which is Rano Kao at the southern tip of the island. Shaped like a mammoth teacup, Rano Kao measures a mile from rim to rim. Its perfect symmetry is fully enclosed by towering walls of equal height. The depth of the abyss from the rim to the reed-choked crater lake is nearly one thousand feet and the vast bowl falls away in sheer drops to the sea on three sides. The inner walls are so steep that grazing animals cannot reach the water, but since men have lived on Easter Island they have descended to gather the totora reeds and toromiro trees that grow there.

Crouching atop the knife-edged ridge separating Rano Kao from the sea is the ceremonial village of Orongo where primitive men lived in subterranean stone dwellings. They made hundreds of strange stone carvings, and conducted the frightening ritual of the Birdman. The cliff falls straight from Orongo to the ocean waters. Offshore lie three tiny islets. In the stretch of sea separating the cliff from the islands, young men tested their courage and often surrendered their lives in their desire to swim across on reed floats in search of the first egg of the year, to attain the designation of Birdman.

Rano Kao is striking, coldly beautiful, forbidding.

The smallest crater, Puna Pau, lies inland about three miles north of Rano Kao. The physical difference between these craters is great, but the difference in atmosphere that each creates is even greater.

Puna Pau rises from lovely rolling countryside reminiscent of the Irish heath. It is on a high plateau and a major portion of the island can be viewed from its rim. The crater sides are of bright red porous stone and it was here that ancient craftsmen carved out huge cylindrical forms, many of which still lie abandoned in and near the little red crater. Some of them weigh as much as thirty tons. A soft and friendly sanctuary in the highlands, Puna Pau is a gathering place for hundreds of grazing animals.

Abandoned topknots at Puna Pau

Rano Kau

THE MONOLITHS

Rano Raraku

THE MONOLITHS

Rano Raraku is simply beyond the comprehension of modern man. One wall of the great crater is of solid rock that towers above the surrounding fields. From the inner and outer faces of this wall unknown men carved hundreds of thousands of tons of stone.

The first impression reveals only the brooding shadowed face of a great cliff, sliced and gouged, pitted and hollowed. As the eye adjusts, a seemingly random configuration assumes recognizable form. Suddenly a colossus is revealed! A stone giant sixty feet long stares sightlessly into a stone canopy three feet above his eyes! Now there is another monolith, even larger, whose form has just been roughed out. And another. And then you see it all. Tier upon tier, a gigantic layered abstract bas relief of monster men. They lie in their niches one above the other all the way to the very crest of the ridge. Some lie athwart the slope while others, nearly upright, lean back against the wall. Each is fused to his eternal bed, mummified in stone before his birth. On every level are stone roofed benches, the deserted crypts of other giants who were freed and somehow transported down the slope.

Some of the figures are finished in every detail and the stone has been cut away around their bodies so that the only point of attachment to their resting place is a narrow stone keel. A few more blows from the workmen's picks would free them. Fifty-three Moai are still a part of the quarry wall.

The impression of sudden cessation of the enormous project is startling. The roadway leading from the quarry is littered with abandoned figures. Everywhere there is evidence that the ancient stone workers suddenly threw down their tools and never again resumed their work.

But most of the great monoliths were born, freed of their stony berths and transported to the gentler slope below the quarry face. Here they stand in disorderly ranks and attitudes filling a vast sculpture garden that was intended to be merely a temporary storing place. Here they wait, a hundred strong. Some are buried to the chin in the soft earth while others lean crazily and still others tower tall and straight. All stare eyeless at the rolling ocean.

The figures are huge and the awesome effect created by their vast bulk is amplified tenfold by the arrogant power so apparent in their expressions. Each figure, though carved to represent a specific personage, is characterized by a mien of imperious scorn expressed by thin cruel lips and a haughty upraised nose. Their glaring, black-shadowed, eyeless sockets follow the visitor's every

Unfinished Moai, Rano Raraku

movement. There exists at Rano Raraku an electric atmosphere akin to the tense, dark, waiting period that precedes an August storm.

The abandoned Moai of Rano Raraku were never meant to remain forever, half buried and eyeless, on the lower slope of the great crater. They were created to take their stand shoulder to shoulder on the hundreds of great stone platforms (Ahus) that rim the coast.

The giant stone bases were not merely stage settings for the most effective presentation of the Moais. The original use for an Ahu was to provide burial vaults for the high-born dead, and since each fronted a temple square it is reasonable to assume that in themselves, the Ahus were objects of worship.

The solar orientation of the earliest Ahus is precise which leads scholars to believe that the builders were sun worshippers who had more than a superficial knowledge of the movements of the heavenly bodies.

In the earliest Ahus the colossal blocks were tooled and shaped so perfectly that a blade might trace the perimeter of a ten foot stone and never find a place of entry.

The design and fit of the stones at Ahu Tepeu for example, are of an elegance matched only by the constructions of similar walls found in the Andes of Peru. The stones are much too large to have been chipped, fitted, removed, and reworked. Each had to be engineered, measured and completely dressed to exact plan before assembly. There is no sign of chipping after they were laid.

The craftsmen, working with clumsy stone tools, took such pride in their skill that they added decorative niceties far beyond the structural requirements. Each stone bellies smoothly forward in a curve so perfect that it could be a segment cut from a sphere.

Many of the Ahus are over two hundred feet long and contain the bones of many chiefs. Whether the original builders or only later arrivals visualized the great burial platforms as bases for Moai is not known, but in many instances the first elegant stone work was buried under tumbled additions of uncut stones.

Long before European arrival the great culture ended and by 1850 every Moai that graced an Ahu had been sent crashing face down into the dirt. Whether this was done by warring tribes as an indication of disrespect for their enemies' ancestors or by mutinous slave workers is unknown. We are only certain that they were not toppled by the forces of nature, but by the hand of man.

For over one hundred years no man had seen a Moai in its original position, but today some of the Moai have been restored.

Ahu Tepeu

Moai at Vaihu

Ahu Tahira, South coast

Ahu Taki te Moa

Stone work detail; Ahu Tahira at Vinapu

Ahu Tongariki; Moai was rolled over by a tidal wave in 1960

During their stay, Thor Heyerdahl's archeological expedition completely re-constructed an Ahu at Anakena. Using only those tools and manpower that were available to the original builders, the archeologists then placed the Moai on the Ahu. Although the red stone cylindrical crown from the Puna Pau quarry was not added, it can be assumed that it might have been originally placed by levering it up a temporary stone ramp and tipping it into position.

Dr. William Mulloy, an American archeologist from the University of Wyoming, was a leading member of the expedition. He has repeatedly returned to Easter Island and continued the rebuilding of the Ahus. The magnificent project at Tahai has been completed. It includes an Ahu on which five Moai stand. Two other Ahus at Tahai are each crowned with a single Moai, one of which wears his original topknot. Professor Mulloy has restored the platform and erected seven Moai at Ahu Akivi, one of the few located inland.

Ahu Akivi

Moai, Ahu Akivi

Moai, Ahu Vaiuri at Tahai

Moai, Tahai

Moai, Ahu Akivi

Ahu ko te Riku at Tahai

Ahu Ature Huke at Anakena Bay

Ahu Huri Arenga

Tahai

THE PEOPLE

Sebastian Pakarati Ika, Mayor Pro Tem

THE PEOPLE

The islanders have enthusiastically contributed their muscle and skill to the reconstruction and the work will continue as international funding becomes available.

The modern islanders' skill in handling the monoliths seems instinctual, perhaps because many of the 1,100 residents are descendants of the earliest arrivals. The physical characteristics of the people are diverse, and any general description of their appearance is difficult. Facial structure and color vary from Polynesian to Caucasian.

The pace of life and the friendly warmth of the "Pascuanese" is in sharp contrast to the industrialized societies of this computerized age.

The people seem to lack only the often annoying trappings of more "advanced" cultures. There are no television sets, newspapers, movies, no phones or traffic or pollution or drugs or crime or hunger. There are no paved roads or private vehicles. A good horse can be purchased for $8.00 and everyone rides—often three on a horse. Since there are four horses for every resident, this seems strange until it is understood that horses are over-burdened only because it is just more congenial to ride two or three together.

There is an ease of living and a friendliness of manner and a great lusty good humor. There is a sense of fun and gusto apparent even in church. Five hundred voices shake the rickety frame of Father Melchior's church every Sunday morning at the 8:00 a.m. mass. Everyone from nursing babies to octagenarians comes to church. Tail-waving dogs wander between the pews renewing friendships. Those people who don't care about going fishing on Sunday arrive at 10:00 o'clock and the straggling remainder attend the 3:00 o'clock mass thoughtfully timed for those who attempted too many Pisco Sours at the Saturday night Sau Sau.

In addition to a bit of Pisco and sometimes some wine or beer, typical party ingredients include lobsters, fish and often a whole roasted sheep that "wandered" from the government sheep farm and was "rescued." In an average year 4,000 sheep just disappear. When questioned about this phenomenon, the islander shrugs and explains that they probably drowned while attempting to swim to the mainland.

The party guest list is flexible but always includes dozens of tethered horses, the ubiquitous high speed dogs and lots of children.

91

Everyone knows, likes, and depends on everyone else. There exists a most sensitive and practical interchange of goods, services and food. If a man has luck fishing, he will distribute the surplus catch to his neighbors. He is building informal credit with a man who keeps cows, another whose watermelons are ripening and a third who can make electrical repairs. Refrigeration facilities are inadequate and this system of immediate distribution when food is available is the perfect answer to the storage problem. Until a very short time ago barter was the sole means of trade and money was hardly used at all. Mainland food staples, clothing, wine and household necessities are scarce since a ship arrives only twice a year.

Family ties are very strong. Groups including great grandparents and infants often share the same house. Children and the elderly are much loved and welcomed for a meal or a stay in whatever homes they wander into. No one seems to know or care what time it is.

The friendliness, hospitality, and interest in visitors is gratifying and refreshing. The novelty and pleasure the off-island stranger experiences from this outpouring of warmth and good humor is tempered only by a nervous fear for the peoples' future. How much longer can this unusually delicate small society maintain its individuality and values against the press of an approaching wave of visitors displaying the paraphernalia of the outer world? It seems inevitable that the seduction must soon begin. Ancient values and traditions and a uniquely casual way of life will be exchanged for a radio station, newspapers, telephones, and jeeps. It seems sadly inevitable that the residents of Rapa Nui will be homogenized into the 20th century within one or two generations. It is distressing to speculate that Rapa Nuians will probably fare no better in a new life style than did the American Indian, the Eskimo, or the Australian Aborigine.

Isabel Berta Pakarati Tepano

94

Maria Tekena Hei, the last remaining daughter of king Atamu Tekena

Augustin Teao Riroko

Leon Tuki Hei

Aurora Espinoza

Victoria Rapahango Tepuku

Ricardo Tuki

Napoleon Paoa Paté

Father Melchior

THE MYSTERY

THE MYSTERY

No one knows how it all began. There are questions as to who the first arrivals were and what port they sailed from. Why were art forms of such magnitude ever attempted on the world's most remote outpost and what purpose did they serve?

Were the workers slaves laboring under the lash? Were the original residents enslaved by an invading group? Perhaps the invaders overwhelmed the populace not by force but through their own fears and superstitions just as a handful of white-skinned Spanish equestrians subdued the mighty Inca nation. Could the situation have been reversed? Were emigrants captured by the original residents and forced to work out their lives in the quarry and along the roads?

Were the builders free men laboring out of fear or reverence of their Gods or respect for their parents and Chiefs? Why did the builders carve larger and larger statues? Perhaps the competitive spirit was of greater importance than is generally conceded.

We do know that other early monumental works of man such as the Pyramids and the Great Wall of China were built by vast hordes under vigorous control. Manpower was drawn from whole continents and more men were available to supply the material, transport and assemble the finished work. Still more men and great acreage were needed and available to produce food for the huge work forces.

But Easter Island is tiny. How many craftsmen, plus workers necessary to sustain and assist them, were active and for what length of time? Where did they come from? How could the island produce enough food? How was it all possible? Perhaps one day the answers to these questions will be known, but the chances are slim.

Reconstruction of history without the help of written materials is very difficult. There exist only about twenty records of the early period. The records are called Rongo Rongo and are in the form of wooden tablets. Translation of the intricate carvings on the boards has defied the world's experts for over 100 years and today not one symbol is understood.

Archeology depends for its accuracy on many sources of information. In addition to written records, an important key used to decipher the puzzles of the past is the spoken word passed down in the form of legend.

Though legends are often distorted or dramatized over the years, trained specialists are often able to piece together a chain of events utilizing the legendary information to bridge the gaps between the physical findings.

On Rapa Nui this link to the past was practically severed when nearly the entire population was destroyed in 1862. Therefore, the world's awareness of Easter Island dates from the arrival of the first European visitor. The first decipherable written records were written in a ship's log on Easter day in 1772 by the Dutch captain Jacob Roggeveen. His notes were filled with wonderment. They conveyed the first knowledge of the existence of the island to the outside world. He noted that the natives wore little but tattoos, were friendly and unarmed and lived in reed houses. Their only tools were of stone. His men shot thirteen natives when they attempted the pilferage of a few hats and then he sailed on at the end of the day.

No European appeared until fifty years later when the Spaniard, Don Felipe Gonzales arrived. He marched ashore with a large group, including two priests, and before he left he planted several crosses declaring the island a Spanish territory.

The next traveler to appear was the famous Englishman, Captain James Cook. His visitation in 1774 was distinguished by some communication with the residents through a Polynesian crew member who was able to decipher a few phrases of the local dialect. They learned that the giant statues were memorials to earlier chiefs and important religious personages.

The Frenchman, La Perouse followed in Cook's wake in 1786 and remained for the usual one day stay. He tried to help the inhabitants to start a farming community by landing some pigs, goats, and sheep as well as seed. The islanders promptly ate the lot.

An American visitor was next. He came to steal and kidnapped twelve men and ten women to colonize a seal hunting station off the Chilean Coast. All twenty two jumped overboard and drowned in an effort to swim home.

These exploratory visits from the members of more "civilized" societies were culminated in a virtual extermination of the entire population in 1862. Seven Peruvian slave ships, after celebrating Christmas, sailed for home with one thousand islanders shackled in the holds. Within a year nine hundred had died of hunger and disease in the Guano pits of Peru. Only fifteen of the thousand ever returned home and they brought yet another gift from the outside world— Smallpox. Before long, the once great society had shrunk to one hundred and eleven miserable souls, hungry and sick.

The first report that attempted to record more than a superficial impression was written in 1886 by Mr. Thompson, paymaster of the American frigate,

Mohican. During his ten day stay he recorded what legends he could gather concerning the first settlers' experiences.

The earliest European, Roggeveen, did not arrive until the century after the great age of construction ended. The reports that he and his followers wrote were based on swift impressions of small parts of the island. Their writings, while spell-binding, did little to illuminate the happenings that occurred prior to their arrival. It was not until archeologists began their systematic investigations that any factual accounts of the past became available.

The first modern investigator, Katherine Routledge, landed in a small yacht in 1914. Her time was spent mainly in surveying, mapping, and cataloging many of the visible features of the land. Although her observations were valuable she unfortunately had insufficient time, inadequate equipment and manpower with which to complete work that might have led to definitive conclusions. Routledge's writings transcended the purely scientific, so moved was she by what she saw.

"In Easter Island the past is the present, it is impossible to escape from it; the inhabitants of today are less real than the men who have gone; the shadows of the departed builders still possess the land. Voluntarily or involuntarily the sojourner must hold commune with those old workers; for the whole air vibrates with a vast purpose and energy which has been and is no more. What was it? Why was it?"

Following the Routledge expedition no further important work was attempted until twenty years later when a French-Belgian group arrived. They concentrated on collecting folklore and studies of rock carvings and stone works, but attempted no excavations.

The bits of writings of all of these visitors made it possible for laymen and many archeologists who had never seen the island to develop their own personal theories concerning the past.

Among the more fanciful suppositions in and out of vogue is "The Archipelago Theory." This theory holds that Easter Island was a great burial center serving a large nearby land mass or group of islands that have since disappeared beneath the sea. This is often expanded and combined with the "Lost City of Atlantis" concept in which a great city lies beneath the sea. However, underwater surveys have established that other land masses never existed in the vicinity.

Extremely titillating is the currently popular "Man from Mars" explanation. This theory maintains that outer celestial visitors came, constructed, and went with nary a souvenir of their visit left behind. Why a people with interplanetary capability would chip out immense monoliths with miniscule stone hand picks is unexplained.

For the latest and most authoritative listings of known facts we are almost wholly dependent on the findings of the Norwegian expedition led by Thor Heyerdahl. This was the only large-scale professionally staffed and fully equipped group ever to attempt excavations on the island.

During its stay, Heyerdahl's group excavated several Moai and Ahus, explored caves, intensively studied pictographs at Orongo, analyzed the prehistoric dwellings, conducted pollen and carbon tests and investigated many objects and places heretofore uncataloged. In addition, they demonstrated the method by which the great statues were probably transported and erected.

Thor Heyerdahl, in his writings, gives full credit to the enormous contribution made by Father Sebastian Englert, a Catholic Missionary who lived on the island for 35 years. Although not trained as a scientist, Father Sebastian greatly enlarged the then existing body of knowledge of the past. Englert's analysis of the folklore combined with the scientific findings of the Norwegian expedition provide the first authoritative answers to some of the questions about Easter Island's mysterious past.

The findings of the expedition overhauled the shaky structure of myths, half truths, and superstitions that comprised the information available prior to their arrival. But archeology is a painstaking, time-consuming endeavor and the large team working steadily for a year could only scratch the surface of the myriad secrets that lie hidden in the thousand caves, beneath the ancient houses, and within the Ahu crypts.

The Norwegian expedition findings have been assembled in two volumes of encyclopedic proportions and definitive scientific fact. These can be found in scholarly institutions throughout the world.

Since the completion of these volumes, new facts have come to light as a result of extensive testing of carbon and pollen samples gathered during Dr. Heyerdahl's investigations. Dr. Heyerdahl has graciously summarized these latest findings to give us new insights into the history of Easter Island. Answers to some of the larger questions may be the subject of speculation forever.

Tiny Easter Island stands apart as a monument to the skill, industry and dedication of an earlier society. Here there flourished a tribe of men possessed of a strength of conviction—an unshakable belief in something so powerful that it is beyond our comprehension.

Petroglyph at Orongo

Ana Kai Tangata, (cave where men are eaten)

Petroglyphs at Orongo

Makemake carving near Rano Raraku

Stone carving, Anakena

Makemake carving near Rano Raraku

Stone carving, Anakena

Entrance to stone dwelling at Orongo

HISTORICAL SUMMARY

HISTORICAL SUMMARY
by Thor Heyerdahl, Ph.D.

In these days of moon travel when continents are creeping nearer to each other, even Easter Island is on the threshold of being drawn into the realm of sober reality after generations of mystery and isolation. A fairy-tale island is emerging from obscurity and as it is getting closer to all of us it begins to show clearer contours.

Not much more than a decade ago there was no airport on this remote speck of land. Located as it was far away from any shipping lane, a visitor had to find it with his own boat unless he was lucky enough to secure a berth on the Chilean naval vessel that made about a week's call once a year. Although Spanish is spoken today by everybody, a couple of decades earlier any foreigner would have had difficulties in conversing with the few hundred local islanders without a Rapanui interpreter. Another eighty years before, these islanders had never heard of Christianity, cannibalism was still in vogue, and any visitor would step ashore at the risk of his life.

Father Eugène Eyraud, who ventured ashore in 1864 as the first missionary and the first European to settle among the islanders, would hardly believe his own eyes if he could see the friendly Easter Islanders in their Sunday garb flocking into their village church today. He wrote to his superior upon his landing: "The people are horrible to look at. They are menacing, armed with lances, and most of them are naked. The feathers they wear as ornaments, the tattoo, their savage cries, give altogether a dreadful appearance."

These savages, a hundred years ago, were living in isolation on a barren little island dotted with the vestiges of a former civilization: everywhere were ruins of temple platforms built from enormous stone blocks meticulously shaped and fitted together as if they were merely cut from cheese. At the feet of these splendid terraces lay giant stone men toppled over on to their faces, and in the precipitous quarries of a dead volcano lay many more colossal busts uncompleted, some with nothing but unfinished, blind heads emerging from the descended silt. Captain Cook, when visiting the island in 1774 stressed the local lack of leadership and organization. He referred to the spectacular stone constructions as "monuments of antiquity," and stated that "the present inhabitants have most certainly had no hand in them, as they do not even repair the foundations of those which are going to decay." His companion, the scientist Forster, observed that the inhabitants, "destitute of tools, of shelter, and clothing, are obliged to spend all their time in providing food to support their precarious existence. It is obvious that they are too much occupied with their wants, to think of forming statues, which would cost them ages to finish, and require their united strength to erect."

Cook and his companions also pointed out that they saw no worship of the colossal stone statues, and were convinced that they did not serve as idols to the present inhabitants. The islanders seemed of a uniform Polynesian stock according to Captain Cook, although all were small, lean and miserable with a language containing so few Polynesian words that even Cook's Polynesian interpreter found most of their speech unintelligible.

Half a century earlier, however, when the Dutch Admiral Roggeveen had discovered the island on Easter day, 1722, he and his companions had found the people ashore still paying tribute to the images. They lighted hundreds of fires in front of the tall statues while prostrating themselves to the rising sun. The Dutch discoverers, and the Spaniards who came from Peru as the first visitors after them, had, in marked contrast to Cook, found white-skinned people with red and even cinnamon-colored hair among the dark-skinned Polynesians ashore. They found many of the men to be of an exceptionally large stature, and out of curiosity the Spaniards measured two of them who were respectively 6 ft. 5 ins. and 6 ft. 6½ ins. tall.

It is significant to note that the two first European expeditions to reach Easter Island thus explicitly recorded that they found a mixed population, as these observations give historic support to a vivid tradition surviving on Easter Island until modern times: Two different peoples with different languages and different cultures had lived together on the island in ancient times. A civil war between them had stopped all work in the quarries and brought misery and decadence to the island, tragic conditions which lasted well into the early period of European settlement at the end of the 19th century.

No European eyewitness had the experience of seeing Easter Island at the peak of its glory. Peace and order must have reigned on the island for many centuries then. This is shown by the almost incredible achievements of the local stone sculptors, architects, and engineers, and also by the total lack of arms in all archaeological deposits prior to about A.D. 1680, when the sudden war ended all constructive work and left the surface of the island littered with obsidian spear points and scattered blocks of buildings and monuments. For several centuries, perhaps close to two millennia, the vast ocean space surrounding this tiny speck of land had given its inhabitants the peace to turn their barren landscape into an almost coherent temple ground, where each extended family had its own sanctuary and its own monuments to deceased heroes. Historic records show that each statue was carved in an ancestor cult to immortalize a king, a chief, or other important personality supposed to become deified after death. They were carved with long pendant ear lobes because the people they represented extended their ear lobes artificially. They were erected with a super-imposed *pukao* or topknot, of red stone, because the people they represented had reddish hair. We know they were carved by normal stone-age men ignorant of metal tools, because their pointed stone picks of hard basalt were left by the thousands in the quarries. They were carved taller and taller as generations went by and skill and vanity increased. The tallest of all were in fact left unfinished or ready for transport from the quarries. The taller they became the slimmer they appeared, but all followed the same prototype: a smallish basalt statue of the supreme god that had been worshipped since the earliest local period by the whole island population. They burned fires in front of this old pan-island image when all tribes gathered for the non-Polynesian bird-man ceremonies near the solar observatory on the summit of the volcano Rano Kao. Since all later kings claimed descent from this supreme diety, they all wanted their monolithic portrait to look like him. The people who had carved this venerated prototype had witnessed Easter Island in its first cultural period, and in these early generations monumental art was far from stereotyped. Our excavations in 1955-56 uncovered hitherto unknown stone statues differing completely from the classical Easter Island type. They included forms ranging from that of a stubby and realistic kneeling giant with a goatee beard and hands on its thighs, to that of a conventionalized pillar-like image with a rectanguloid cross-section, two of the specialized monument types characteristic of the pre-Inca civilization in South America.

The people who started to carve the first variety of giant stone men on Easter Island would hardly have recognized their own landscape had they come back centuries later and found more than six hundred stone colossi, all imitating one of their own masterpieces, towering against the sky in almost every part of the tiny island. Yet it was not their successors who had first changed the appearance of the island. Indeed, great changes had immediately taken place in the very earliest period of human settlement, perhaps the greatest ever. Hermetically preserved pollen, deposited in layers in the bogs surrounding the Easter Island crater lakes, can be collected and identified through pollen borings. Such investigations have recently revealed that prior to human arrival Easter Island was not more barren than the other volcanic islands of southeast Polynesia. The island was in fact covered with woodland, with trees and shrubs that have subsequently been exterminated. Before human arrival a now extinct palm covered the volcanic slopes of Rano Raraku, which have since been sliced into the precipitous naked terraces of the image quarries.

The first human immigrants cleared this forest with fire, and converted the landscape into large fields of South American sweet potatoes. Arriving already as expert masons, they ignored the value of timber, and looked for quarries suitable for shaping huge building blocks and statues from the naked rock. In this early period the settlers even built circular dwellings of stone with openings through the thatched roofs, like ancient people on the nearest mainland of South America, but unlike all peoples on the thousands of islands elsewhere in the Pacific. Before they arrived, not one freshwater plant grew in the rainwater collected in the extinct craters of this remote island. But the first settlers brought with them two useful South American freshwater plants which gradually turned the hitherto open crater lakes into regular bogs. One was the important *totora* reed which was used, as in South America, for building bundle-boats and for thatching houses. Man's arrival is marked in the pollen deposits by a layer containing soot particles from the rain of ashes descending into the lakes as the forest was cleared away by fire, and in later layers the pollen of the virgin land vegetation disappears. Huge stone men began to grow up in a strangely barren landscape covered with low grass, small ferns, and tall reeds. Thus man had changed the face of Easter Island for the first time.

Man has never stopped changing the face of Easter Island. A completely new island is now beginning to emerge as a jet airstrip has been built across the southwestern headland. Tourists are beginning to pour in.

Settlers from the outside world have also begun to enter, while on the other hand many Easter Islanders have chosen to leave for continental Chile. The first hotel has been built in Hangaroa village, and roads have been built widely over the island. Many of the islanders have begun to learn English in addition to Spanish. Continental merchandise began to flow in as a real money economy was introduced. This great social revolution gained impetus in 1966 when the Chilean naval administration of the island was replaced by a civilian administration.

The Chilean government has also started extensive reforestation. When my own archaeological expedition camped in the sandy dunes of Anakena bay in

1955-56, this legendary site of the first island king was devoid of any vegetation taller than weeds bending under our feet. Today a visitor to the same bay will have coconut palms waving above his head. When we visited the giant cauldron of the Rano Kao crater in 1956, the last tree of the *toromiro* forest, that had survived here through the ages of destruction, was so mutilated by the woodcarvers that it was clearly doomed to die, and so it did. This tree, which grew nowhere else in the world, had always served the Easter Islanders for their carving of wooden statuettes and paraphernalia, until every trunk and root had been exhausted in the late 1950's. As a curiosity I had collected a few seeds from the last dying tree and presented them to the leading authority on the Easter Island flora, the late Prof. Carl Skottsberg. He planted the seeds in the botanical garden of Gothenburg, Sweden, and three *toromiro* trees came up just as the last specimen on the island withered away. Danish botanists brought seeds from these trees back to Easter Island as part of the Chilean reforestation project.

Not only are hundreds of trees once more growing up from the scorched ground where they had once been burnt down and destroyed, but one by one even giant statues are rising up to resume their former pose on old platforms from which they had fallen. This restoration of image *ahu* and other early monuments has been led by Dr. William Mulloy and Gonzalo Figueroa, two of the archaeologists who witnessed how twelve Easter Islanders re-erected the first giant statue during an experiment conducted for our expedition in 1955.

In the future, the Easter Islanders, having already left their huts of stones and reeds and joined the rest of us in the houses of global civilization, will be able to look out of their windows and experience the strange atmosphere of bygone days. Days and nights when sun and moon shone on some of the strangest and most impressive mausolia human hands have ever created: monuments raised in a fanatical effort to commemorate what are now long-forgotten men.

Ahu Akivi

Printed at Scroll Press, Danbury, Connecticut under supervision of Susan Latham, production manager. The 300 line screen negatives were made by Thomas Watkins, Jr. The design is by Fred Picker; the type, Optima, was set by Dumar Typesetters, Dayton, Ohio; the paper is Warren's Lustro Offset Enamel Dull. The edition was bound by A. Horowitz & Son, Clifton, New Jersey.